LOVES
Poetic WATERS

KEYERA AUMEYERIE BEY

Loves Poetic Waters

Copyright © 2021 by Keyera Aumeyerie Bey rights reserved. No part of this publication may be reproduced, distributed, or transmitted in any form or by any means, including photocopying, recording, or other electronic or mechanical methods, without the prior written permission of the publisher, except in the case of brief quotations embodied in critical reviews and certain other noncommercial uses permitted by copyright law. For permission requests, write to the publisher, addressed "Attention: Permissions Coordinator," at the address below.

For details, contact the publisher at the address above.

Copyright © 2021 by Keyera Aumeyerie Bey ISBN: 978-1-716-18503-8
Printed in United States

Keyera Aumeyerie Bey

Loves Poetic Waters

Preface

Poetry was my escape as a child ever since I knew how to write and express my emotions in form. I went through a lot regarding attachment and love itself as we all do. My outlet became poetry and art. I started out with general diary entries and enjoyed having something to commune with regarding my day. In middle school it transpired into me and a group of friends deciding on sharing our daily feels with a "friend" notebook we decorated with our names and separated sections for the three of us. This we would pass around during class changes and at lunch and write in it sharing secrets and more. I noticed my pieces were more emotional and felt that I took to it more than they did, it is funny to look back on. I then decided to continue in my own books and on a beautiful social website that was popular at that time. I filled that with many of the love poems you will get to read in the pages ahead. This book in particular focuses on my relationships and the poems I wrote about each individual, it is personal, but the time has come for me to share since I do not do much of that when it comes to my art. This took a total of 10 years to finally put into play and publish one of many books. In between two chapters is a missing piece in my journey so intense it deserves it's own book so I would love you all to look forward to that piece soon to come and enjoy this piece just the same.
Thank You

Table of Contents

CHAPTERS	PAGE
Title Page	I
Copyright Page	II
Authors Page	III
Preface	IV
Table of Contents	V
Note	VI
Acknowledgments	VII
Teenage Daze Premature Love	1-11
Traveling Hearts Eyes	12-20
Triggered INception Love Abyss	21-46
Wings Fling Passing	47-55
Intermissions Messages	56-73
Karmas Love Try-Angle	74-90
Back	91

"I am defined by love...
Love is my Instinct...
Love is me.."
-Raine

Acknowledgements

In life we have people that become major aspects in creating who we are in the present moment. These experiences can be days, months or even years. Time doesn't matter much as the connection can seem forever, like you have always known each other when you have only just met.

I would like to thank Mikas Dillard as she had the most impact on many things in my life, the good, bad, and eccentric. I learned a lot about what love is and is not through you. I appreciate your presence in my journey. I hope all is well with you and your endeavors. I always wish you the best.]

I would like to give a special thanks Epiphany Sholar as you Kueen gave me space to be myself in ways not known before our time together, our time was art in raw form, an ethereal escape to a place never known, and will never be forgotten. I am always here for you. Strive and never look back, you deserve it.

VIII

Teenage Daze Premature Love

Prelude

This chapter of my life I was experiencing the need to feel a different kind of love, something rebellious and free, a caged bird ready to fly. An introduction led to a whirlwind of emotions, A deep connection that opened my mind body and spirit to an unknown world. In my Sophomore year in high school, I met Mikas. She was captivating by sight and her energy was like a drug I never knew existed. My favorite movie was "twilight" at the time, so I am not surprised to have manifested such an experience. It was steady, fast and intense. High emotions and boundaries removed we were young with unknown expectations. She was aware of a lot more then I was at the time. I was unexperienced in street smarts but felt the need to dive deep into something I was pulled away from as a child subconsciously. The street life, getting things from the dirt as we say. I wasn't getting the connection I needed from my family and as children we go and search for that missing piece outside of ourselves. She was into things I presently wouldn't approve of but because of her own upbringing and traumas I had seen beyond that and chose to love her unconditionally. Nights of car rides and sneaking into each other's homes. Parties and getting into trouble, smoking and drinking with intoxication as our guide. We were both running from reality and escaping into our own separate wonderlands together. In this chapter you will walk with me through the ups and downs of our roller-coaster. Our love bitten escapades and delirious pain.

First Time

The first time I heard about you....you sounded great an I wanted to meet you The first time I met you, you were inevitable, beautiful you I wanted you but was blinded by a hold a couldn't get from The first time I was with you, you blew my mind I love your personality The first time you called me your voice over powered my heart deep freezing my feelings then an there The first time I hugged you I loved it your warm embrace melted my whole body The first time you kissed me...Lol it needed work but the next time our lips where ready and molded perfectly into each other's The first time we were alone with each other it went on an on our time seemed like it was never ending The first time we admitted our love for one another it was a moment that could have lasted forever The first time we picked our song...we cried tears together because the feeling an meaning was deep and true As our feelings grew so Did our anticipation for something bigger and better.

Unnamed

MY mind racing Heart pacing Thoughts going back to our hours of love making Heated passion Developing sweat Blurred moans Both dripping wet Shaking bodies Heightened breathing Our Love Now Stronger A New Type of Feeling...

Yes ...I want you Yes... I'm afraid more now than I've ever been Yes. I need you Yes...you are something I've never felt I'm addicted Yes..iloveyou

the love I have for you I can't disguise the love I have only you can see with your eyes our hearts intertwined a love so divine you are mine anxious, even just to hear your voice it's like my feelings no more have a choice they jump and dive off the highest cliff Ive never felt love like this a never-ending roller coaster my heart goes up and down my heart beats deep for you with the loudest sound

Mm

Don't be the one..dont be one of them, don't break my heart cause I'm sure u will be the last one to have my heart..I'm suffering from a serious condition of continuous heart break, please be the doctor to heal and repair me, love, me take me into your arms and give me your heart in return to love, let me love you, care for you, and show you things you've never seen or felt before, take my hand and let me guide you, trust me as I trust you, fall an just know that I will be there to catch you.

What Was This

What Was This Was this all a lie, a fairy tale, I wish my eyes and ears deceive me for my heart crumbles at the sight of those words and die wen u say them, I am tired, tired of fighting for someone or something that is not mention to be, tired of finding things out when it's all ready to late, baby I'm already in love, y do this when by our design we have planned everything, by us going through the same thing and saying how were so tired of the same fucked up shit, well I am beyond all measures, I thought we would change that together.

Unnamed

I just Wanna spend some time with Ya So I can say some thangs to Ya do some thangs to Ya Put that pain on Ya You know how we do Making love with the tunes Enjoying the different views Some moaning and screaming too Late nights and early mornings Whispering our sweet nothing's Feeling good in our feelings Put that ass to the ceiling

I want you to make me call you daddy as you pull, bite, and hold down my body Make me scream and release my most clandestine things Open my world through my six senses Meet me in outer space in the darkness Don't think, just do play out your vulgar scenes Sex tapes and cunnilingus in every thought-out place... I can't wait....

I see you in a better place but you stuck running the same race You say you Tryna get away but you worried about saving Grace I'm a little bit upset watching you in this position Read back on what was said in our composition...book Stars are aligning and you sitting there crying How I know cause I'm in the mirror and I'm not lying Hate to say it but I'm still feeling it... in my aorta Hard to get rid of something that's twinning it...no Morta Angels come and tap on my shoulder and say don't forget I don't Wanna listen cause our past...running shit I'm just venting...

Guitar song for her

Guitar song for her love it is what I have found she stands there across the way with a face that is remarkable she is beautiful with every flaw she has outstanding without even putting forth an effort amazing with everything she does the way she walks, talks the way she looks at me, it sends me away to a place Ive never been, I love it undeniable, I trust her with everything she has my heart and the key my eyes set forth to give upon you my hands molded to have your hands placed into them my ears tuned to only hear your voice my lips sculpted to be pressed against yours my heart shaped for the key that you have you have words that could change my life eyes that tell a story I want to live lips that speak inevitable words my soul is tied to yours we do a dance that lasts forever when I look into your eyes I feel like in home with a touch you send me deeper than before you're my eternal flame you keep me burning burning with love, lust, and life we burn together love as deep as an ocean but has more meaning than Outerspace bigger than the atmosphere when I see you all six of my senses are awakened you fill every cell in me with life baby, you are like my own personal brand of heroine....

The Ends Near

I hate you. You seep through my pours like mildew Yea I hurt you, but you hurt me like birth do Didn't Wanna let go ...I let go. But now you're in my peripheral Sore eyes you caught me without head proof Iloveyou easy out holding it in is where you find proof I in end want no alleviation from what you could do What we could pull through Love pulls through ... Why...why hide what is felt inside Yea it hides but it creeps up the outside of the inside of you Putting up a fight Beautiful post I see your might You make me Wanna climb your thoughts and sink into the spill of your ill Sing ...songs of high meals... crease the edges of my seal let me know when you heal My mind escaping into a landless field Catch me on this flight pass the pipe ..the next hit leads me to your cry Find me swiftly sailing through Love seas finding the right current for me never ending sickness of this deep sea But it holds me...memories of what was haunts me like the dip of your soft curves Perfect picture perfect stitcher you fit to my body like milk meets honey Mama you pull back on me like the last key

The Ends Near Cont.

Thinking oh so loosely of me only for a moment but that's all you need You play a nice game indeed But all of you I profoundly read Don't reply sorry if I interrupted your sleep. But I'm sure you're up counting heartbeats...having that one moment you so loosely need Past heart's knocking on your door that you wish were no more I send you back to when the Red walls mirrored the floor Christmas lights flowed and incents where the door Music played the melody and the room was filled with you a dash of me, I said nothing ..the air filled my nostrils ...I said nothing my thoughts purified by you...I was pronounced speechless with your headdress I was a mess...my best I had only wanted to be filled with the feeling of you and that 10 sec window which felt like forever ago your eyes made my thoughts slow my heart flow under the radar monotone You burrow so deep into me. you haven't released

Conclusion

I learned a lot from Damikas, she taught me freedom in a sense of expression in certain ways. She was more of a catalyst to my journey. The pain I experienced through the breakup I went into what is called now a dark night of the soul. In this space its heavy and I experienced dark thoughts, disbelief, attachment, fear, hate, overall wanting to hide away and run from life itself. I needed to get away from all things that we filled with our presence. That was my hometown as a whole. I removed myself from people, places, things, while still attaching to the thought of maybe. With that thought I kept the line of connection open with minimal contact to her because that love that was felt was irreplaceable. I also wanted the opportunity to present itself if I had another round in this rollercoaster. Which I did when I moved to Columbus we will cover more in a later chapter. We had a connection that started slow but steady and kept this interesting momentum that became a confused friendship. We could talk about any and everything. There were no secrets between us, well on my end at least. Intimacy still included that caused havoc in her relationship at the time. I honestly didn't care because what I thought I felt at the time overtook morals and values. I always made space for her no matter my circumstance. We stayed in contact as we continued our separate lives in between time she made visits that always turned into pain at the end, but I adamantly kept a space for er seeing her greatness and wanting the best for her. No matter the pain caused. I still haven't realized at this point of my life that once a [person shows you who they are, believe it.

Traveling Hearts Eyes

Traveling Hearts Eyes

This part of my journey I began traveling to different cities and states to get away from all the turmoil and pain from my previous chapter. I came across a fellow fish Tiana. We vibe and what felt like a movie for a short time became an experience. Intense emotions and heat through a long-distance relationship formed. It was a child like love, and we didn't know much of what we wanted. It was fresh and when two Pisces collide it can be steam or waves. We tend to go with what we feel, good or bad, in the moment and overreaction is evident in this type of relationship with inexperience. Nonetheless there was a mutual understanding and fluidity that allowed closeness and authenticity to prevail. I went to see her, and it felt amazing going all that way. Pretending and roleplaying as friends to evade parents, erotic moments in front of her friend, kissing in the rain and lasting pictures on the Amtrak. These moments will never be forgotten as a dream was brought to reality even if it wasn't a lasting fairy tale. My appreciation in our short bus ride as it led me to the fullness of who I am today.

T.M.W

When Fishes Swim

Her heart Found the key to mine Time slowed One again I walk with time Nothing feels fast Everything feels right I've begun to feel her Even though she's not in sight I love her But I'm afraid true enough That things won't last Once things get tough She has a breathtaking smile Personality to match Someone I won't be letting go I've found my perfect catch Only time will tell I intend to heal all scars T.M.W I take your hand as we walk through all doors.

Unnamed

My lips through your heart I kiss your soul I knew from the start You'd make me whole My heart serenades to you I endure love once again I can't wait to get to you to feel you hand in hand Your words, they secure me in and out no doubts or frets I no longer have a reason to pout let's see how good this gets Baby you stressing When everything is a blessing Don't let this be your discretion Try to learn a lesson Keep your head on the heavens Write it out, all your ambitions Goals and aspirations and how to finish this mission Anything irrelevant just dismiss It Daddy you got this I'm Right here by your side to hold your hand through whatever we gone hold our stand Show those who thought we couldn't, we can .... It's me and Her. 7.24 Daddy, you've done something to me Your love is running real deep through me You voice Laying over in my mind Speaking words that are so sublime Heartaches No more felt on this heavy heart You came in and made a fresh start Time has now slowed and I can breathe easy It's crazy how you're so far and I still feel in sync I have not had the great feel of your gestures but how I feel now I can only fathom When we're together I'm honored to Call you mine for a lifetime Never let go once your hands in mine...

Unnamed

I just Wanna tell you baby that I love you... Making sure you know I wouldn't put no one before you Mind contemplating on how to make you my wife I plan on there being an US for the rest of our lives Shit has been hectic for me let me be honest I'm studying your love Now I'm hooked on Phoenix Best believe I'm gone give you all that you wish for But if not I will show you so that it means more Excuse my worries And accusations My past walks pass my door causing hesitation I'll love you until my heart grows old Even then I'll love you in the warn heavens while my heart is cold Your eyes seep into my heart You digging deep found the word restart Words easing all my pain you found a way to relinquish all strain, your love resides in my veins....

Saying bye bye to the old sky Time to see the world on a new high. See you later haters, Fake ass instigators Bout to hop on my pencil, writing me to this paper on my own shit, higher mind, I'm the shit This time I start, best believe I won't quit yaw stay working 9 to 5 Just to stay free and alive I'm gone be working for myself, no radar on my life... Just doing it for me and mines

Unnamed

Baby... let's kill the pandemonium with our silence Then slowly rise our tone into something thuggish no violence Let me have a day where there's no interruptions Only our bodies and tongues gone be having discussions... I miss you. Like I already kissed you... And don't let a bitch try to diss you I'll protect you Won't neglect you Bitches out here half stepping Blind to what's in their hand Not knowing how to take that stand Baby I'll do the best that I can I love you unconditionally Understand what you mean to me You filled a void so empty You got me completely You got me feeling good...too good

All For You

Soft words roll as you take me whole Once again, we let our love spin Deep within we find our grin and let it sink into our soul Nights like these I take to appease Fall back on the count of three and now we are able to see... Flash...Starbucks is where I wait 5 mins away and of rather stay Flash...your voice ruptures my silence And I'm embodied in amazement Flash...you stand so tall and your Everything caresses my all Flash...our energies collide and I don't have nothing to hide Damn...why must I go. Tears felt like years and now I'm on my way home, but it never stopped there It was just a tare of what I am Now aware of.. What I was scared of... When I once feared love... And here I see love Here I feel love... Here I can be me... Understand who I am when I say I am me... Intertwined with so many pines and all I want it endless time... I want to catch my final one way to you... Hopefully that's where I'll have my last DeJa'Vu... -omIrie

Releasing Thee

I released thee after year three and looky here we are in sync once again oh my don't let this love end unless it's the infinite bend fluidity I see in thee don't let my eyes speak for me my heart flails at the thought of we I just want to BE all that I ever was plus all that I really am so that there is an understanding that is so deep that it is felt through sand ...meet me in the astral...

Conclusion

I was the cause of the ending. Fate interrupted and steered my vision completely into a new direction. I happened to go into a family dollar and had eye contact with my twin flame. Leading to days of enchantment and removal of my current reality. We had a previous problem with her kissing someone while out and I wasn't too happy but in no way did I intent on causing a severing of our relationship. Fate stepped in and did what it always does when change is needed. This totally remove the fact that I was even in a relationship. Somethings just can't be explained.

Days after coming down off this high I remembered and felt so bad. A walk and a long conversation concluded this part of my journey. I couldn't go back and don't know how it could've gone any other way then then me not intending to give someone my number in the first place maybe. Even then, the only thing that could've stopped something that seemed so otherworldly and fated was no eye contact.

Triggered INception Loves Ethereal Abyss

Prelude

A Regular stop in to store and a meeting of two souls eyes turned into a storyline of passion and art unfolding. Ever looked into someone's eyes and felt like nothing outside of you two mattered? Or even felt time itself had stopped just for the breath of two beings could be felt in each other's heart? This was that and these moments lasted in every encounter. We moved as if time was nonexistent. I moved in in less than a week as we made brownies and planned our ascension together. Pushing each other as we made love in ethereal realms while music became our melodic transportation. I was her alien, and she was my escape. This time was shortly interrupted as the energy filled parties around and the enviousness of such a strong connection can be sought out and destroyed to the oblivious. We had to move in with her friends and things were a rollercoaster after that. The peace we built became a battleground for infiltration from those around us. We held up people around us and faltered within our own relationship. Time became more real as rent and responsibilities piled upon us. Drinking and Parties became our newfound escape. Lies and infidelity snuck in from every corner. Pain hit and I drowned in the overwhelming waters of others creation.

Unnamed

I did find a better you Stumbled into a Family Dollar Now we take in each other's view Almost like DeJa'Vu mind fell into constellations of you She understands my soul Willing to take me whole She touched my brain Like an internal vein She removed all pain I feel no strain Around her I can be at my worst She keeps me grounded to earth She appreciates my worth Love formed beyond earth Names carved in stone No longer feel alone in a filled room I love how we swoon... I had an Epiphany about you...my Kueen

our silence together only tells how much were thinking about our next move, what to do next, what she's thinking, how she feels, this moment, how I feel, us. so much roams through our head we can't make a move, we just need to let go and let things happen, don't think, if that happens, we can do everything and anything we always wanted to do with each other.

Lone Kuyen Meet Lone Qyng

I'm tripping because I'm slowly sipping on this tea that I once had and it's driving me crazy because maybe just maybe you are my forever lady and with that information it's making me uneasy because love for me isn't no satisfactory... steady dazing to days from way back when my love found it's end... I'm talking forever feeling less that I was all just because...I settled for less, she gave me stress and pain, but you can remove depression... every night having to dream about sleeping but only cause the lights are out...thoughts about ending a life worth living because to me losing love was the ending...why? Why do I latch on so tightly to love? Because when I needed it most it was nowhere to be found so when the smallest bit came my way I tried to keep it in no sign for escape...I couldn't love myself because I didn't know what love was for me... barking up the wrong trees, trying to sail a ship made of imagination across mud seas...with the misdirection of intuition...false love leaving me blind, just going along for the ride...now I have my chance to see love for what it is... free falling knowing you're there to catch me... scary cause it's all I've been wanting and needing...I can see "me" , and be "me"...I can sleep...the best sleep I've had in years...I feel you feeling me...I love that you are reading and learning me...consoling me... you already have a part of me no one has foreseen...I love that you give what I give...it's remarkable to me. I feel free...I can't wait to live life with you... walk down that aisle, speak them vowels and say I Do... because I Do wish to spend the rest of my life with you...My Epiphany...

Quoted sentiments

This Goddess of a Kueen has my mind on fleek

Lips... Not just any Hers... Soft like kitten purrs I Wanna play a sweet melody on your guitar...solo I take you on and make your trumpet hit the highest note Pause. A breath of smoke hits the air scented of your hairs ...I pluck each string as we try to fight the stare

Cont.

She got that...forever soul That don't let me go baby when I look at you, I can't believe your my (wife) let alone that I have someone like you in my life you make me feel amazing inside, a feeling I thought I had before but Ive really never had until I met you you make me feel brand new, you make me want to do anything and everything for you to make you happy, make you smile, laugh, cry tears of joy

Unnamed

I got a confession Of my slight obsession When emersed in your congression Its more of a mental session See you obtain this kind of heaven That welcomes me in your presence I'm floating on cloud eleven and hoping you won't hit seven I'm prying out my eulogies Come seek the sea with me Release the powers of we Third eyes with Yang and Ying Lets learn to sing embrace insightful springs Let go of boastful rings Reach enlightened means Gather all Kings and Kueen's Unleashed our vibrational streams...

Unnamened

I Wanna trace every crevice in your creek and let our intertwined ooze seep and all over we shall leak..they Wanna take a peek but other eyes will only cry as the depth of our love sings. Roar speech but soft and settle like a humming bee. I seek thee my Kueen

Unnamed

Can I say how beautiful your soul is...how not being in your presence you are able to still make cheeks wave to the other but when in your presence the lightest touch of your feathered glimpse can make the doubt sink...you..Kueen..deserve more than eyes can see more then money can buy. The sun and moon from the sky..you care so deeply and it's a beautiful gift heart of gold you know super women don't have anything on you..do you know how much you are loved? You make the wheel of the world turn..and your expression of your lip lined words mixed with the makeup and hair curls are like raindrops from heaven..pleaser forgive me for my words pour from this backed up Whirlpool of say it say more... -raine

Truth

Truth is I want my soul inside you Crawling through your veins making your feelings see through You got me out past my curfew I yearn you Soaking through my soil and planting your seed beneath my thin layer Sprouting through my veins in a fine coil You so pure...so sweet. And just for me now we grow this tree... our tree Filling all dreams and fantasies I see something in you...the same I am Tryna bring outta me My golden breeze My Kueen I Love you My Epiphany

Hot faucet ran cold

I had an Epiphany... my did she catch me in a link...made my heart sink soul fell in a brink she made me think. Less... I had to push my ink...miss oh that kiss you made me trip on our never-ending grocery list...and then we hit a twist. high five and tie died our everlasting mist. Too bad it wasn't forever... Wish you were more than a lesson my beautiful blessing you are forever in my heart. You push the start and jumped the next cart all because we both fell short. . I forgive you..I just wish you would forgive yourself for your own health release that stealth and breathe. ...be that Kueen so maybe one day you shall match that Kyng. And sing that beautiful song....ILoveYou

Cried my eyes out...
I hope you know I really mean it all

Yes. You done with me Lost it all in just a count of three Sorry you have no clue what's it like to be me I tried I tried. But what's destined for me No matter who I gave the keys People screwing my mind using my weak links I wish my shoes were big enough for two Then maybe you'd understand the battle I go through... Love like this just don't end I keep coming back...coming back...

Unnamed

I had an Epiphany... my did she catch me in a link...made my heart sink soul fell in a brink she made me think. Less... I had to push my ink...miss oh that kiss you made me trip on our never-ending grocery list...and then we hit a twist. high five and tie died our everlasting mist. Too bad it wasn't forever... Wish you were more than a lesson my beautiful blessing you are forever in my heart. You push the start and jumped the next cart all because we both fell short. . I forgive you..I just wish you would forgive yourself for your own health release that stealth and breathe. ...be that Kueen so maybe one day you shall match that Kyng. And sing that beautiful song....ILoveYou

Unnamed

What were your intentions I live in a pained dimension Your love has stricken Was it really goanna work? Were you really past the hurt I was ready to out you first Constantly feeling controlled What's right will take hold the good ones don't let go It's our destiny on three Kuyen and the Qyng but how to make this bird sing?

Reaching for this epiphany Tryna get hold of release But it won't cease the Reason destruction is named the beast I'm fighting my beast Taking it off the leash Mama here go the keys This time ride don't speak I'm hitting my peak But I need your heat I want this can't you see No rushing let's take this cruise No worry nothing to lose I want you mama I'm a prove Just be patient cause I'm Kinda rude Baby I caught you like the flu Something so E.T I'm forever soothed There's this girl and all a nigga Wanna do is give the world But how do you get out of twirl You accustomed to nothing short Wanna feel you every day be the Dom-and to your Sub-ply Relax girl get high just vibe Sitting on the ceiling peeling the pipe

Unnamed

Oh...miss epiphany did you forget I was at your house night after night Only want back to give our love a night Yea, she was at home waiting for love to come home but she was wrong I was at your front door and you... Mad for what? We were planning and you and TC still wanting to fuck but was I mad nah because I had my hand but yours was hidden, I was just the muffin man ...can't bring a beach to the sand...

Waiting

Waiting...anticipating our ever-calling arrangement of love statements Fired from the hesitation I'm soaking in our passion you tele my pathy and leave me savvy... Words ready to flow as soon as you knock on my door ...see you in my seyet and now you act like you don't know. This game we play is far overdue time to release my cards I played enough I'm folding through. Love isn't as deep as mine you pay but don't play with the time.

Ignorance is a crime when bliss is kept benign... Undermind me...I overstand to inner stand you. You are sinking ships and keeping this cold grip on my crypt with the knowledge of the golden sip. All held within the sight of that settle yet deadly...the time has been stopped steady kiss... It's you I miss all else I dismiss. But don't get me wrong. Easy is a song but my worth is where it belongs... Find me in the lost... -Raine

Obsession

I crave your misery it sinks into the depths of me I sometimes neglect thee because you grasp something so kept of me Time goes on and now I'm wept of peace Who knew time could be so leashed I'm waiting for thee the one Who sees Not only that but can find my crease The one found out among the bees We I Wanna speak of we not me Not I not a sigh in between we unless I'm between thee Three times three equals six no six no six I want three Times the peace ...time for relief time to eat words of wisdom pearl this wisdom yes I'm talking about this tree Where's my Kueen I'm waiting to be crowned Kyng ...

3/22

Saw her today. Very enlightened soul. Energy still rises as we lower uneasy vibes. I do love her...deeply... Inside and out... I just wish she'd see this... Welcomed with love and unexpected receiving. Intensity filled all four corners and the air sounded like Raine drops... Cycling in and out of our dimension of depth covered by caution...but We wish to be free..I sEYEt sea you being you. Happy and free... Whether by her side or floating with me... I love you and where you place your feet... Your dreams match yOUR eyes... We locked in our visual as the reality we hold seem to subside... I see as your tears fight to hide... Your soul doesn't let it be jeopardized by the figmented reality ... Unravel that vail and reach up high...

Tethered

You...lit up when you see me. Face and soul...submission to the heart...don't become blinded by fool's gold Our moment seemed like a century. Dream filled with relief by ecstasy you craved the depth of me... Intuition speaking louder you run, and I continue to chase after, and I will forever follow footsteps you anchor the key and thine know what's best... This love story for told. I'll fight ill hold breath to take hold. You are my Kuyen...tis the tears to see your heart be wasted on words of falsity ...tethered to the goosebumps that had had been dormant waiting for your hand sent. Tethered to your alien features that rise when your Kyng reflects you! Tethered to the truth that surfaces when no one's around to tilt your crown! Tethered to the communication that holds no words all in the Look of the eye we sink depth in OUR soul! Tethered....to nothing because all of it is something even when you detach because the reality is you are discovering what is...truth...iloveyou... -Raine

You

You...were the fuse... Some say a muse, but you gave me the blues Thankful it was you...earth wind and fire as you soaked what was sewn... Love forbidden... Lust driven... Only sought out what could be done... maybe? Where was your focus...ready to run... Poetic with my mood swings and you knew this... Love is an exciting passion that courses through veins in a red colored fashion... Love is the beautiful ups and downs in one picture and there is no figure that could capture all this in one. We live it through raptures... Could you handle it? What fairy tale entails the beauty without the beast..I look back and see that that's a selfish thing...close to greed... Good in which we feed without the realization that perfection is benign amongst all things...but I sought perfection in you. In all that you are even you embedded yet seen hidden scars... Yes, I SEEN you and the tears you dropped because the sensitivity you have soaking up and letting the darkness hold you down from the clouds that would ultimately bring you up...baby life really does not suck...and a beautiful soul like yours a light so dim and yet you still seem to grin. This fights you can win...tall order to fill not in measurement but in sight on red or blue pill. Letting go you'll find your fill... Don't let those eyes turn to shadows under the florescent powered dyes.. -Raine

Truth

Can I tell you my vision? I was on this pedestal and you in the pin...we were tethered my royalty did not bring us an end...my Kueen energy does not lie I fell to see. But now I have seyet...I was selfish, and my emotions led the direction. Please forgive me ...instead I choose to let my heart lead and lay my mind to sleep. Princess and prince ...the fire to this water now we make steam...heartbeat hear my soul speak I will put myself last to see you use your wings mama let me be thy king I welter to your guidance I know nothing I said I know nothing I am left..I have only your breath to breathe...I forsake thee, and I am here to be redeemed.... -Raine

Up hill

You are easily on mind when the clock strikes 9 And I'm wondering why we're not intertwined Crazy is I'm feeling fine as you plaster your laughter And koi magic on social medias caster... cause I'm the divine and you are mine silly rabbit the games I've mastered so I play the mime ...I sit back cause I'm in alignment with time Sooner or later, we'll be singing our alien lullaby...

TF

Our twin flame love story put on hold to experience different categories which turned out to be a bit gorier. seasons past in the back of our minds on replay subconscious wishes to have a replay and I must say my forgiveness goes a long way yes, I would rather you be my third and final love cause the second one was such a short phase, filled with steam and misconceived trauma and rage testing our Gangtsa to move on to better days... we escaped the race and now intervention comes to stir alignment cause outside of us there is only confinement and together we reside within the golden shift needs to rock the kids I said elevate the kids and bring forth passion into motionless institutions in the mind that is!... baby yes, I love the fire we make but more over I love the passion lit in our heart and eyes that brings forth love in our aura. And heaven descends down to bring order in just for our path to brighten and cause more of.... the same -Raine

Unnamed

It turns out you are the poetry in my veins... The thousands of years I waited just to write again You were the muse in my past life Now I'm reaching for you to be my wife ...in this life Draw a blank and I don't care if it doesn't sound right Tell me truth that the feeling isn't true, and I'll retract my sentence And remove my heart from your mentions But be sure of your decision Because I promise I won't reembark on this mission 11:11 on the clock you are the vision Weather you know it or not we will see the fruition Of our dreams once spoken for and the love we are missing Let our energies collide in the physical...there we will find the truth beholding no need for words Eyes piercing through long awaited souls ... Heart beats come to pass, and one touch brings amass Euphoric implosion felt between the two Energy vapors disturb the surrounding Environment we ascend into our celestial view... I'm ready Kueen and so are you... -Raine

P.S

You will never be abandoned by me...love stuck on you like a eucalyptus tree.... sap me up on the count of three...love is forever between you and me

Conclusion

After too many lies and conflict within the house and our relationship I spiritually and mentally was pushed beyond my limits and escaped into another dark night of the soul. A twin flame relationship is a hard break when not meant to come into union. It is very painful. She left me in my depth for another person as an escape. I still tried to stay but she sent me on my way. I Went years without speaking but the direct link will forever remain in the ethers. Even if it doesn't happen in this life the beauty and the beast energy felt within this connection will never fade into the abyss. They say once a poet falls in love with you, you will forever live. Which is true. At the thought I could continue to write poetry on her. She will Live forever one way or another, we created art together. She sings and writes poetry and can draw for days. Very talented in her being. Her power and freedom lie there. Kind soul and burdened with things around her, but she knows what she wants, simple and misplaced maybe but she goes after it. When she sits and removes all the noise the flower waiting to bloom will become the rarest of them all. My Twin.

Winds Flings Passing

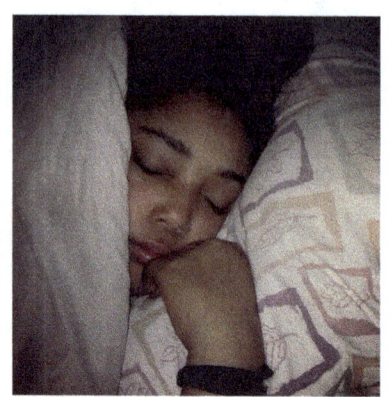

Prelude

In this part of my journey, I moved forward and started attracting experiences that only reflected the healing I still needed to heal within myself, with turmoil and flings that showed me the lack of self-worth and inconsistency I had within. This time of my life I was on the brink of an internal shift. That will soon show my next level of lessons ready to internalize. Each of these women had a highlight on certain parts. They all though seemed to bring in a third party of some sort. I as well did in some instances. Poly was a thing in the second encounter but turned out I only learned that when in poly there must be a foundation with two individuals then the expansion can happen. But without that strength in the two starting individuals the possibility of manipulation is high. I ultimately did not mind as I had found a peace within as I was shown the outcome of the situation and appreciated being spared honestly. One situation decided to bring in my Twin for an escapade, but she knew nothing of what that was and her being a catfish we had the last laugh. I did what I could in that situation, but she lied about who she was and many other things. I bought this woman a ticket and everything. Man, it was a foolish move but hey you live, and you learn right.

Unnamed

This world so delusional Take Ya as Ya usual, you're beautiful. Not knowing where the beauty lies, they think it's in the cuticles I Wanna take you out this cubical Learn what makes the world so unusual ...Be the living proof ... feel the world through our roots Speak the truth. run wild be the wolf Fall back... be free. let me be the wind flow through Ya leaves Yang to Ya Ying Arms to sleeves Spark the chi Raise the heat You got me so fluid I can smooth the beat What can I do to take you outta here Make our own biosphere Slow time make it all disappear I'm just Tryna clear the Rearview mirrors Maybe if they don't see they can hear us? Lay the knowledge through the clear void Burn the currency make it hypnoid Get rid of all these androids I can see it in my Clair..Voy...Ance Its almost time to do our dance Sing our song raise our hands Flames dancing with the trees All at once we take our leave, I'm ready if you ready let's take this leap

Honesty

Honestly. ..Ive been crushing on your existence since our light body's met Quiet it's been kept but my thoughts seem to be so erect on the thought of you on your smoothness edgy enough to sooth this Take a hit of me...then count to three What does your sore eyes see I have carnal visuals. Simply put it becomes spiritual ...my femininity glows as the Kyng in you shows...my interest peaks You I would call elite all because of how women you treat... I want you to cool my heat Align my chakras and cross my dimensions Ive become slow with decisions But I want to delve into all that you are My midnight star I don't want to own you I want to own with you Fill my vibes with new Dig into the depths of my fear Embrace the darkness that's clear Engulf my intellect decode the sects Spark that intensity get high with thee What are you afraid of? Let's sync our flows without clashing Use needed action to change what's happening Become one of many by being few of plenty My lovely antidote lets be the anecdote Namaste

-Sage

Slighted Catfish

Amanda Marie Price...love shines effortlessly through your eyes Don't let the world make you cry Times like these we run and hide No longer have to worry How you're seated I'll give you all that is needed You are a Queen still Undefeated Can't wait to see you soon so I can see it...

A what could be poem see the flow isnt really flowing it was a mishap of forced poetic rap maybe i could mend my fruitfall mind finding crumbs in my souls depths...i found nothing...

Shadows dance

Clears throat so... She wonders.... I do to.... So, I tell her.... I Wanna know the real you.... It may seem like play but it's non the less real I wonder. So, does she.... but my vibe, she does not kill....
Lol

I swear to earth I Wanna fuck the shit out of her intelligence. ..unf....she got my mind speaking some kind of Spanglish my unknown danish I Wanna creep up your intellect. And dive into your everything on the count of three...take hold of my release...fuck my brains out I'm screaming for this peace. ...piece.... of you I want you on top of me... hold me down I Wanna call you papi....carnal thoughts this woman is craving something so demented...hear my cry I Wanna pry on your cloud nine don't be so shy my expression so sexual cause I'm feeling inside...damn you left me on this cloud high...

Failed Triatholon

Constant....I'm sick Tired of this mind playing heart tricks I'M SICK I FUCKING QUIT I'm Tryna play the good role Evil guiding the shift I'M FUCKING HIT Nowhere to run I'm wishing the list Tryna get my fit Head cold it switch I DON'T WANT NO BITCH Kueen status legit Nah she quick to flip Mind control hit to miss I'M SICK OF THIS SHIT Wanna be my mami but can't finish the lick Thursday I'll be ready to pick None left but one If so I'm leaving a ton God has the gun Past is the past Now my future is won Whose the one It might be the Cancer son Cause Leo got the Leo And the Scorpio isn't got the juice....

My Rush to See Her

My rush to see her heart raced when you said those words "meet me somewhere" ugh my heartbeat, hard and loud I hear it beat through my ears can feel it through my chest I can't take it... I clench on the seat belt like never before speed limit has no meaning at this time heart feels like it overflows with feelings it's too much... I hold my breath, barely breathing until I see your face my life will come back when I wrap my hands around you and your lips seal my heart I breathe again...

Let Go

Let it go, if locked up Close your eyes, throw yourself back I'll catch you, just like the butterflies Hold you, embrace the gift Your divine beauty, there's no share In dusk I'll hide you and never return you back

Conclusion

This ended my external search for love and all the fairytale things we see in movies that are ultimately for that purpose only. I took stock of where I was in my life and the situations that I was attracting and decided I wanted to manifest a different reality for my future. I removed myself from all situation, people, places, and things and went on to unlearn and relearn what life is and what it meant for me. This took a time of solitude and new energies. I met myself and found out what love is and what I wanted from it. In order for me to really grasp what love is I had to apply self-love and learn that for myself. That included acknowledging the good, bad, ugly and beautiful within me. Accepting who I was uniquely and moving according to that as a whole. I had to remove things within me that allowed things that I no longer wanted to experience, like self-worth issues and standing up for myself, out. Not saying no and many other actions and thoughts and reinforce those positives parts of me that supported my endurance and upbeat outlook and strength. I was grateful for the people and experiences Ive had up to this point in my life and what they taught me about myself and needed to learn and heal from. Also, the parts of me reflected from them that I ultimately thought I lacked within myself.

Intermissions Messages

Prelude

This part of my journey I went on an internal walk. It was the moment in time right before I started my biggest journey within of knowledge of self. This was the preface before the deep transformation occurs at different points in everyone lives. This was letting go and going through complex emotions of each of my past encounters with different relationships, choices I had made. The rollercoaster of denial anger, back paddling, confusion and more that occurs when you only have space and time to reflect and face the truth of things. Here in this next chapter, you will experience my inner conflict at this point in my life.

confidenty lost-sabrina claudio

Sentiments

It's all in how you pour your wine Demented
but its whether you feline or intellectually
fine

Wishing

That Love that love that love that holds on forever that love that you feel when you wake and is in your dreams when u sleep that love that everyone needs that love you want to breath that love that makes your heart ache because it feels just that good that love you can't believe you have that love that has your mind never on earth that love that you can feel running through your body that love that has your heart beating a different beat that is the love that I can't wait to find

Missing

My whole body wants to reconnect with you. When we have our time alone, I want to talk to you about everything that's happened. While I undress you slowly and trace every inch of your body. Whisper sweet nothing's to you while you continue to try and keep your breathing under control. I want to make you remember how I can stop you in mid-sentence and have you saying "Yess". Only because I know how it will make you feel...

I

I miss The curve of your hips The taste of your lips Escaping sighs As my tongue thrusts between your thighs The musk filled scent of lust filling the air Your hands on my head, fingers tugging at my hair.....

Where

The clock strikes 12 and I'm lost for words I said I'd move on to another soul Wishing someone would accompany this heart so cold I push ahead when I'm being pulled by you I can't ignore my heart when it overruled A love so strong it courses through my veins Trying another soul only causes more pain I'm linked into you on a level unknown Even my horoscope says this is wrong Don't give up Cause time is near If you run away now, what will happen Is your fear Love is my motivation but only your kind The love you give is a love so Devine I feel imprisoned but it's a sentence I want to serve Everything brings me back to you like the ultimate curve A spell has been cast upon me to never leave your side Talking to others only last so long then it dies I hate this I hate it cause I have no control What have you done to this heart that was once so cold I've thought about the what ifs and maybes Leaving you behind and carrying on my lively Everything disagrees mind heart soul and body The world shifts backwards for me considering such thing

What Was

If there was a way for me to say the things, I need to say the Right way....me and you fuck the other two .... damn it feels like a repetition but in this division it's hard to make a decision.... but me I know What I want I know What I need and it's definitely you with me...till this day I still shake When We first encounter mind goes blank temp raises higher. I don't want anyone else, No one else compares, No one else can get me wet..they don't know How to give me your stare... that glare that weakens me all over...only to make me want to be closer...to you

Once Upon A Time

Guilt, pumped with every heart beat Your voice, it makes me weak Past chances I fucked up I hear you, have I lucked up If I had one more chance to show you the real No lies, no secrets show how I feel My heart was locked in an invisible cage Thought I was in love When I was Really in rage You said I deserved better Loving me is a pleasure I chose a lesson instead When it was you in my head Looking at the stars I seen your smile Wondering what we'd be if I'd took the extra mile Love mistaken for lust Heart zeroed in on us No chances left I pull out the rest Time will only tell as we're closing in on, he'll Now you're happy all by the hand of a man Wishful thinking that it was only until I could grab your hand, I express myself now, Cause in person I'll be speechless You will always have a place in my heart...I'm nervous as you read this...

Heat

Seeing your face pop up on my timeline brings back fatal memories from our timeline I'm glad we went our separate ways cause who knows what kind of pain you would've caused these days You sicken my soul while taking me whole you are a monster under my bed The boogie man in my closet watching me sleep plotting on my head I wish I Could get you out of my thoughts that creep up on me I wish I could stop hating you because it's weakening me I wish I would've listened, so I wouldn't be stuck with this regret Maybe I could forget you if you would just burn my bracelet Why do you carry me with you while you say you don't care Want nothing to do with me but my ring is what you still wear Don't come after me when you have fell on your last luck I can't help you, I won't be there for you cause when I needed you, you left me fucked You are the worry in my veins The pain that remains The reason I can't write nor sing You killed me, the light that shined so bright You cornered me, took away my reason not to fight You are my unfortunate heartbreak Put the knife through my back without making sure the next breath I wouldn't take I can go on and on because to me you were never ending Now I'm sitting here... hoping you aren't living.. If you are, I hope karma is setting in Reminding you what you did...

Unnamed

Why does after all this time of not caring I feel a slight taring in my aorta.

I thought that feeling was cordless creeping down into my solar plexus what's the meaning of this...

back and forth on this blurry arrangement is it time spent in each other's energy or the feeling of feeling lonely...??

why? when this lonesome being is so use to lone wolf seams.

Unnamed

Deep connection, high on the prime election. I mean ...it's time to let go and move onto another flow, this one is a no... who would've known, it's like I enjoy suffering, feeling my heart buffer. Stomach flutter, pain is what I muster. Disgust her.... living in the past, force clinging in the last, minute. Never late but time escapes, soul ready for a release. Emancipation on the scene, gold eyes and cleaner dreams. Tired of the entrapment... negative thoughts causing this elapse-meant... But I vibe and try to stick it live.

Prize

Looking no longer no need to feel somber, heart set upon this feeling I'm healing no wonders. Baby go that soul glow beautiful just hear her moan. Something so special she knows what she wants, captain of her own. Damn what a blessing she teaches no lessons, hard at hearing, but she tests me and reassess. What a message The way she walks you feel dog bites slowly walking with lions her height dripping, she humble. No pride

2

Sitting back and I'm letting loose.
I said I'm locking my bow and arrow, its set I got it cocked.

On you

Waiting on your cue yes baby ima shoot Hope you have the points to size it. Done with the fantasizers. I plan on having you ride...long nights and great moaning rises

No games are being played baby join me in this maze and watch the craze...can you manage the wave.

4

Yea see we are flying out to Paris, see caution flares...sailing on the seas hat tipped and I'm thinking about having you say please...cross Ya knees
She my inspiration heads up she push me to be my greatest. Hood with a lil conservative, she ah blurred line. Majestic and mysterious is her nature she stands strong and wont chase Ya
Her words make chest moves alone she a zone on her own. Shawty wont life one finger and have a squad built and grown. Gotta give it up to her she bad with two D's

Young Blood

I was star struck over green grass searching for homes in empty glass. He had the remedy just for me strike the core of my hearts beat. Used his cunning enamor as his delicacy, Motives behind his speech. I left him entrusting only what eyes can see. He soothed and guided me to his captive scene. Tantrically pressed his energy through my loose seams, toyed with malignant means. A vulture diminishing wanderers dreams. Stranger withing my energetic body I had enough of the touching I make the mistake of letting his tip inside me only to feel death griping for a source from me. He wore the suit so well... Eyes that told beautiful lies with a blank smiling stare. Words that wore uncanny but looked with yearning ears. Tears streamed as the dream was over. Full understanding of what had mowed over...I stated the car that once needed a fire and left behind another fallacy of my hearts interpreted wish.

Conclusion

This ended my external search for love and all the fairy tale things we see in movies that are ultimately for that purpose only. I went and began to embark on a journey of truth. I moved and sought after and attracted more experiences that led me to know about who I was and who I am to become. My true purpose in people's life and why I was attracting things that I was. This started my knowledge of self which will be vastly covered in my next publication. It truly deserved its own space for exploration and expansion. I began traveling the world nomadically with other going to different communes and farms and connecting with the nature around me. Meditation, crystals, yoga and more along with healthy eating and healing traumas brought me to where I am today. Everyone should take this journey with and find the truth of self and the reality of things around us. When we do this journey, we realize that everything outside of us is a reflection of what's going on within. As always, we are tested to see if we are actually ready to move forward.

Karmas Love Try-Angle

Prelude

This part of my journey I face a big decision of leaving the states ore revisiting a past relationship that was presented as it had some weight of moving forward, it did not. It was another rollercoaster that I needed to get the finishing lessons in before I moved forward in a cut loose kind of way. I had just come from deep, shaking, penetrating experiences from the two years of traveling, meeting new people and having earth breaking events take place. I revisited this person and went through a three year up and down, in and out ordeal trying to figure out why something wouldn't work and how I could. When in reality some things aren't meant to work, and the signs are there for you all the time whether we want to release and accept that or not. Experiencing someone else's reality when you've created your own can be exciting or drowning it all depends on if it does or doesn't match where you are currently or push you forward energetically. This is the lesson of learning when to let go.

Karmas Love Try-Angle

Seeing your face pop up on my timeline brings back fatal memories from our timeline I'm glad we went our separate ways cause who knows what kind of pain you would've caused these days You sicken my soul while taking me whole you are a monster under my bed The boogie man in my closet watching me sleep plotting on my head I wish I Could get you out of my thoughts that creep up on me I wish I could stop hating you because it's weakening me I wish I would've listened, so I wouldn't be stuck with this regret Maybe I could forget you if you would just burn my bracelet Why do you carry me with you while you say you don't care Want nothing to do with me but my ring is what you still wear Don't come after me when you have fell on your last luck I can't help you, I won't be there for you cause when I needed you, you left me fucked You are the worry in my veins The pain that remains The reason I can't write nor sing You killed me, the light that shined so bright You cornered me, took away my reason not to fight You are my unfortunate heartbreak Put the knife through my back without making sure the next breath I wouldn't take I can go on and on because to me you were never ending Now I'm sitting here... hoping you aren't living.. If you are, I hope karma is setting in Reminding you what you did...

Resurface

I Wanna crease your outline and dip you in the finest wine I said I Wanna crease your divine line and fill the intertwined You've been touched by so much sun Your heartbeat becomes the one Shot through my soul the gun This time I'll fight no run..ing in the woods without you Sight fell now I vibe to go through Fields of the unknown but this I can do Where have you been baby, I see you...

4.10

Now my heart thumping and you pumping through my veins. Thoughts fluid with you my subconscious pulling the reigns...4.10 never left. What if I was searching for you through my aim and became lost through the pain tried to bury you but you grew when it rained. Moms scoping me yea we might be hoping I wane. She always come back and its genuine maybe she feels like woe is the. But her soul is tired she's aspired to run after a materialistic hang glider no way of our path if gold is not what transpires

Memoirs to you

Sweet like honeydew, morning dusk drops on grass blades, can I taste you? Not just your nectar but something much better that won't fetter. your mind and all your in between lines, I Wanna sink into your clandestine unwritten letters, keep our love soft spoken let the walk be the talk eclectic our divine motions. keep me in your mind I know I'm uneasy at times and it's because I have become a soft razored edge through time. but you soften my pledge and cause delirium in my stance, you make me want to be better, trouble with am I enough but as soon as our souls touch the only thing that comes in between are words that don't replicate how much,,,I love you and my actions may look like mildew and it may be because Ive strained away from the real tune of,,what love is, been through Ish and fuck that because it has nothing to do with this but let me say...as long as I'm in your wave your push and pull of mass blue ocean saves the inkling of my tidal pain and cleanses the depth of any strain. battling my ego and fear and struggling to be clear but I do want you, mercury in Pisces so I am better when I'm able to speak to you with what may seem as foreign realities, and my heart beats for the depth of our sea and what that balance would be, and how it would feel to walk in sync with flurry eyes and a mended beat of passionate intense peace,

Memoirs to you cont.

Communication on key and fuck words at that point eyes watch and an ESP is what keeps. and time becomes irrelevant as we watch waves dance under stars and gaze at 1000 feet drops from planes, feisty nights that turn into sexual rage, pleasure and pain music moving our souls as we align our maze.... we get lost but within this we find the gold we thought we had forgot... I have two sides two one ready and the other tempting to step back two...but this is my inner dance so when I become distant, I wish you to grab my hand and take my mind of what is less then ground me into this moment and kiss my lips both sets and set fire to the hearts dance, I have trust issues to, that reflects on why you lack trust too. but I am committed that this we can work through, baby once you have me noting can take me from you and there is my hesitance.... but I am accepting this and slowly letting go of chains and stints to fully engulf hoping the timing will be right for divine sentence....iloveyou like the sun loves the moon out past its curfew just to see it shine through...take me and I will take you...

Taurus

She laid the second stone to the road in the stretch of a home run. The stun. 7 sins she was the last one. Turmoil. Mounted on a golden gun. A decapitated mirror speaks softer so she can only hear you. Mixed as we mingled, I fell repeatedly learning the depth of one lesson tingle. Addiction to lust... what may be... feeling nothing as the light I once saw escaped me...break down broke down to the last round. Fish out of sea drought and manifesting material greed all for a crownless queen. What a one-sided dream. Now I am here recapping and reenacting mentally 7years of fatality...she did a number on me...what does healing and love look like for post traumatic npd..gaslight and projections of self-hatred and abused to get her best means. Pawn on this checkerboard that is played on like chess...distraction to the life that is written on my chest. God bless as I say my final goodbye no more ttyl dont redial my line to singe a final time. I am ready to move on and give God his praise. My heart needs sealing and healing... with you I will not get this peaceful raise...bull head continue your graze...

Love Letters

I've never stopped... Yes, I fucked up... I admit that... Yes, I fucked up more than once... I was young in my actions... Didn't do what I preached... Focused on things that didn't matter... Iloveyou... My heart has been screaming for you... We are a power couple when focused... Get shit done... I got starry on you... Do deep in my fairyland... Found out that's all it is... I know I must work for what I want... All of it... You... Goals... Dreams... Whatever... I Gotta work to have it and keep it... Not easy but damn worth every blood sweat and tear. I used to run from my challenges. I ran... Not anymore... You are a Queen, and I now know what that entails... I'll take my time and do my best and if I fail, I'll try again... Until you tell me otherwise... I love your flaws... All of them ...dreams of you. I Wanna crown you... I just Wanna show you because I know my words are half as much as my actions. No rush in anything I want time to tell... but baby I do want you... I just Wanna take my time. But this just isn't about me... You have a say... If you'd rather me not, then that's coo... But that don't mean I won't stop showing my love and gratitude. I'm just wondering... Did that love for me really die? Sorry I don't think I answered your question... I want you because you are all I think about. You are an artist beyond known measures... I see you. You know what you want... Dedicated and determined Loyal to those you love. Passionate and peaceful feisty and playful... That smile... My oh my... Those eyes make time fly by.

Love letters cont.

Them brownies mmmh... I still remember how you make them... Recipe in my head... The passion in your strokes as you lay that eye pen to your face... I love watching your happiness glow all over... You fit my every curve the only puzzle piece I've had... You care and pay attention to things no one has... Businesswoman. I love your catwalk... How you tip your head and your eyes curl... Lioness nonetheless... You out of all women wanted me happy... Stuck by and tried to understand me... So new to me I didn't explain... I'm an introvert at times... I keep burdens to myself because of the way I think... It's better for you and me... I don't Wanna argue but to converse is another thing... I battle things within... Yes, everyone does but I would rather not speak on my negative thoughts because they are temporary... Coming from my past... But I know that now I must express what I feel. At all times with you... Other people aren't needed in what is between us. And I understand that you have family you talk to about things... To get a further understanding. They are all you have. They have your interest at heart. I don't want to separate you from any of that.

Unnamed

Sorry IM Kirking Truth is IM hurting Tryna be all that I can While bitches Tryna get in Hard to stay on your level Steady getting disheveled IM the Queen to your king We can't be worried about the pebbles Crazy but not by choice Protective hear my voice Bitches start hawking I have no choice but to kill the noise Cause they can't destroy us Trampling on our luck We can't give in We Gotta build this off trust I love you baby understand You the Man besides being a man IM doing all that I can to keep holding you holding my hand Never felt like this Don't tell me you gone dismiss You can't tell me you good After we had our first kiss, it was bliss Trading places back-to-back No worry ain't no slack IM here for you 25/9 Baby we can make it 4 flats IM fighting my struggles Steady Tryna love you Drowning on this old shit Heart seeping in a puddle Mind stay on replay Cause of all that shit she say Pessimism on my grey shades Waiting for the final glaze

Unnamed

I see you uproot in my feed when I last to suppress my leads and think lowly of my dreams. And I've learned that lesson. Don't fall victim to a repeated message. The golden nuggets will elevate your heaven.

All that you've been through you will not have to look for that one. She will appear on a subset. Where your eyes once in your dream met. And no falseness in this gaze silk like milk and this love lingers like haze. This potion of devotion you won't give up felt through all chakras the dimensions line us. And all will be heaven send. A heart turned Lukewarm water from cement. No words needed but the first is I do...you dreamed of her and she dreamed of you...we finally meet again. This shall not end. My love I have yet to meet

Truth sets

I made her my priority. Her love it was hazing. She wanted all of me and gave nothing a sorority . She ensued hate into me made love to the pain she grew in she...mirrored it all and I only saw downfalls wanted to run but her imaginary gun had a hold on me. Fighting demons in my sleep still I protected. Gave what was left in my empty cup feeling only neglection. Hate grew and matched the love I once knew. Now I'm sitting here wondering if ill heal from you. Narcissistic tendencies slightly rubbed onto Now I fear all ill only come into contact with residues of you... good with the game lisp now I hear you speak, and your voice has gone vain sis.

Unnamed

Done with the fuckery and negativity you change only to manipulate.... frenemy You're fading off my radar please just stay far 7 years of mental captivity and shards of glass in my heart... finally, being released from me tears streaming in heat down my cheek. Thats how you know it's real. The catalyst to my life same to stick the knife. Hidden agendas ...covered with glazy pictures.

Question

Ties to my heart do I let you string me along? Fairytale love...white picket fence situations intense and a mending kiss. A god given wish...who am I to intervene this lovely scene or even intertwine my energy when you speak on such things? Torn in between...blessings seem to pause because of a lover's dream. Things become obscene. Things felt deep and alcohol to bandage the seep spirits let the eyes sleep. If you had such a thing would you be so blind to leave it behind? Put myself in your shoes...damn maybe that was me. Cold shoulder and stuck on selfish things and focused on lower things instead of gods given scene. Does this moment count? You cry on my shoulder of your divine love while I wish upon a star for the moment, I am blessed with mine? Or are you mine in a flash because the eyes you are blessed with now shows you the things you should be thankful for now that you weren't in your last? Infinite possibilities my knowing speaks softly to me. Maybe it's you...maybe I'm just waiting on my dream...

Unnamed

Does she have room for me? Mental recession on loves loose needs. Mind fucked and trustless mind blown recert to fuck it...king and queen looking blurry I tread on worry will this be our story? One track mind with a vision of truth falling blind because of a pastime when all in the now showing pieces of my heart and it fears regardless of its purity the falsity will break this art bleeding heart...healing restart love conquers all right? Emotionally unavailable to the love that's ahead in you Wanting to have it all but reciprocity tends to fall askew of two Headlights on this carcus pin pushing in valves' sense Right to the aorta breathtaking this order My look for instant gratification instead pushing through the faults I'm making Mirrors peer from this dimension Time wasting for loves attention Like I'm in the middle of myself and others Not giving up when things get hard or don't go my way I'm not feeling too well Love is clouding my mind Heart reaching out For something beyond time I'm in my own ocean Would rather be swimming in yours The past is irrelevant Need new opened doors... -Raine

Fin

I realized that love we seek is all inside. As cliché as it may sound this line holds weight. We aren't taught as children the value of self-love and introspection. Being objective and seeing things from a point of view that doesn't allow emotions to take over and see the lessons in situations, we aren't taught this. We are taught to self-hate and that if we don't have something then we are lacking and we need to take these things form others, this further pushes us away from the truth. All these relationships showed me how much I loved myself and did not know my worth at the same time. These lessons back-to-back pushes everyone into a state of seclusion. Everyone soon gets tired of the same circumstance happening in a reoccurring fashion. It feels like a deep DeJa'Vu and can cause frustration. The key is to take a step back and take note of everything that has led up to this point. What happened in your childhood that could maybe be causing subconscious decisions that are running on auto pilot in your life. We need to heal these crevices within our soul to be able to move forward and freely at that. Heavy hearts find it hard to do this. Thank you for reading.

Keyera brings you along a timeline of passion and depth within her heart in her book Loves Poetic Waters. Swim with her and feel the ebb and flow of love and the poetry that stems from such intense interactions between two. She traverses Love. Pain. Passion. and more in loves hold. The lesson in it all is worth much more. Why not?

Keyera Aumeyerie Bey is a being who lives by truth. Artist by heart and loves sharing the knowledge she has learned over the years by being a Life Coach and Mentor to those along the way on her path and business. A minimalist and lover of the small things we are gifted in life every day. Her passion is in helping others in ways that uplift and give spark to the next to keep moving forward. Through life's ups and downs Keyera has attained much regarding love, self-love and that of others. Pairing this with her studies of herbal remedies and the benefits of meditation and breath.

www.ingramcontent.com/pod-product-compliance
Lightning Source LLC
Chambersburg PA
CBHW071957240426
43669CB00049B/2713